BLUEHAWK CHILDREN'S ART ACTIVITIES

Parent-Child Series

PATRICE L. BOYD

LifeRich Publishing is a registered trademark of The Reader's Digest Association, Inc.

LifeRich Publishing books may be ordered through booksellers or by contacting:

LifeRich Publishing
1663 Liberty Drive
Bloomington, IN 47403
www.liferichpublishing.com
1 (888) 238-8637

ISBN: 978-1-4897-1834-1 (sc)

Library of Congress Control Number: 2018950689

Print information available on the last page.

LifeRich Publishing rev. date: 07/19/2018

EXPLORING

This book is more ways for a child to explore ideas,
and strengthen their visual experience hands on activities
being coordinated with an adult for success.
They will create memories of the activity
as well as who was the guiding force.
You can add photos of the activities
in progress and add dates and names!

DEDICATION

This book is dedicated to my Dad who built
my first small desk for me as a pre-schooler.
That treasure was placed by the dining room window
that looked out on a dove's bird nest that was busy with youngsters.
The next desk was at the age of ten, placed at the end of the upstairs hall
next to a window - very private for all my work!
Also to my husband who built
my next desk for my teaching creative chores.
The next desks and work tables were created
for my dream-come-true art studio!
Just pieces of furniture... but what a delight!

Another member of the family is included in this
dedication, my Mom. She made sure that I had art lessons
during my high school years.
Our school did not have an art program.
Mom was a teacher and writer who spent her Saturdays
getting me to another town where an art teacher
spent his Saturdays for a year teaching me.

CHAPTER 1

1ˢᵀ COLORING

YOUNG ARTIST
    BEGINS TO LEARN
COLORS,
    SHAPES AND NAMES.

**TREE STANDS
    OR
HANGS**

**GREEN TREE!
RED BIRD! BLACK BIRD!
BLUE BIRD! YELLOW BIRD!**

NEED:
SCISSORS, CRAYONS,
TUBE GLUE,
CARDBOARD - CAN USE
PIZZA BOXES.

IDEAS:

✂ ✂ ✂ ✂ ✂ ✂ ✂ ✂ ✂

Coloring:

Let a child color back & forth or up & down or scribble - even outside the line!

When you cut out the birds - it will look great!

Lots of praise in any effort helps the child explore these new ideas!

HAVE FUN!

Cutting:

The line outside of the bird image makes it easier & faster to cut each out - (see next page).

Fill inside line with blue or green or yellow around feet - different from bird's color.

Recycled materials can be used:

pizza box cardboard & string.

American Crow

Color Black
Color around feet Green

American Cardinal

Color Red
Color around feet Green

Wilson's Warbler

Color Bird Yellow

Color Blue around feet

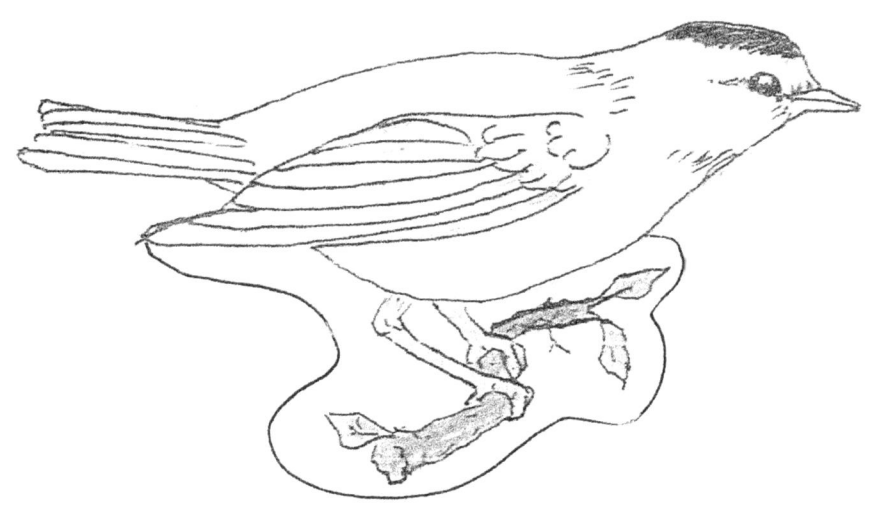

Color Bluebird Blue

Color Yellow
　　around feet

Mountain
Bluebird

FRONT

HANGING TREE

COLOR TREE GREEN
Cut Out.
Glue to
Cardboard.
Glue Birds
To Tree.

BACK

COLOR TREE GREEN
Cut Out.
Glue to
Tree Back.

DIRECTIONS FOR STANDING THE TREE

USE YOUR RULER TO DRAW A LINE
DOWN THE _CENTER BACK_ OF YOUR TREE.

COLOR BOTH STANDS (following page) GREEN
CUT OUT BOTH STANDS. GLUE BOTH TO CARDBOARD. DRY.
CUT OUT.
HOLD TOGETHER TO SEE IF THE _POINTS MATCH_. TRIM.
LAY THE STANDS DOWN.

PLACE YOUR RULER ALONG THE LINE & FOLD UP.
GLUE THE _WIDE_ AREAS _ONLY_ TOGETHER.

GLUE THE THIN AREAS TO
MIDDLE OF THE TREE BACK - BE SURE THAT THE
STAND ISN'T LONGER THAN THE TREE!
DRY FLAT.

TREE ARTIST IDENTIFICATION LABEL

Glue to Tree back:

TREE WITH BIRDS
MADE BY: _____
DATE: _____
AGE: _____

PRAISE THE ARTIST AND THE ARTIST'S WORK!

PHOTOGRAPH THE ARTIST
AND ART WORK TOGETHER
FOR YOUR SCRAP BOOK!

TREE STAND

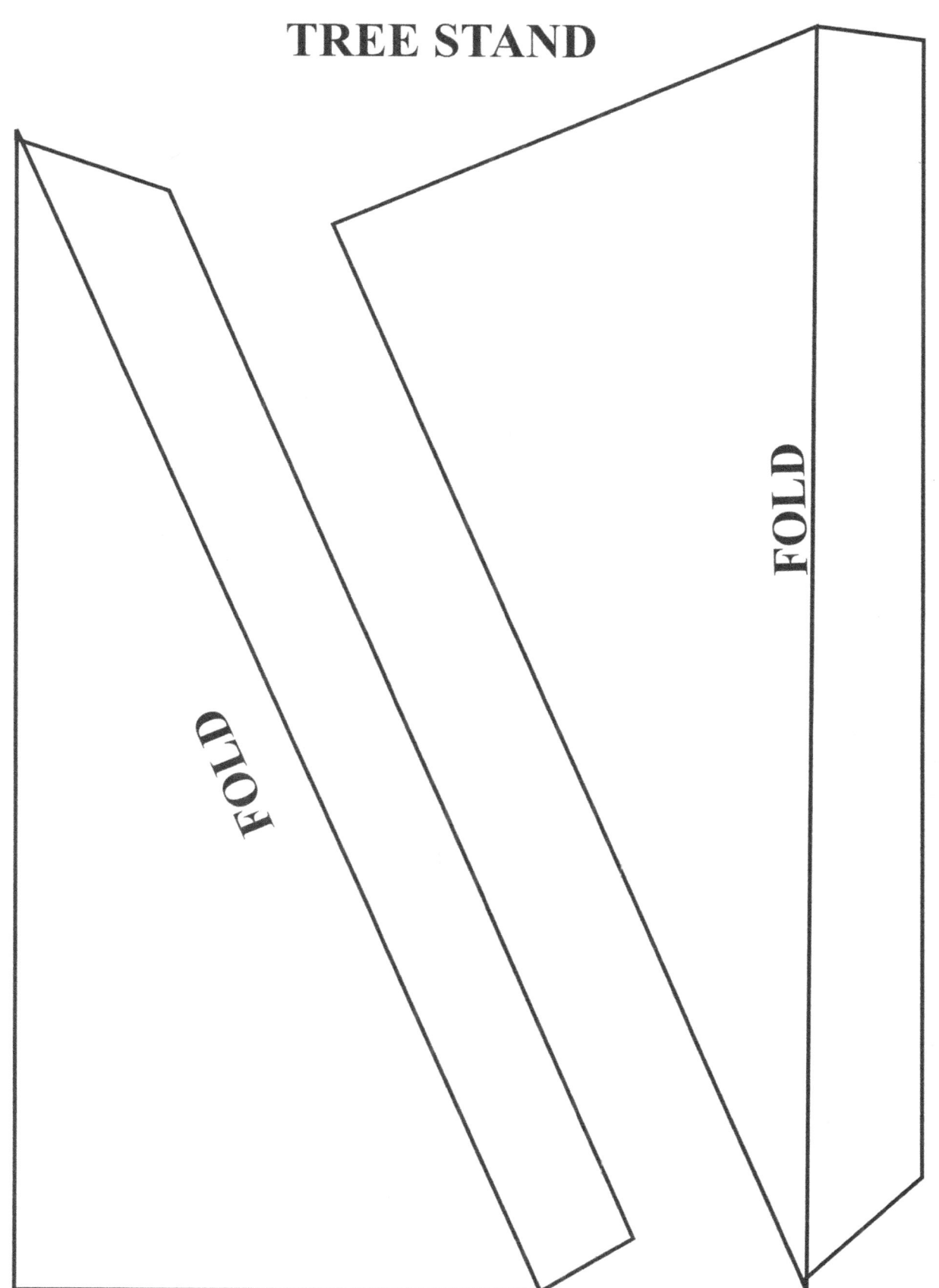

FOLD

FOLD

CHAPTER 2
1ST MOBILE

CLOUD CLOSE-UP
WITH PAPER CLIP
FOR HANGING.

NEED:
CRAYONS
SCISSORS
CARDBOARD -
   (CAN BE
    PIZZA BOX)
LIQUID GLUE
TUBE GLUE
YARN

Tie String to
Paper Clip
(See Mobile
Guidelines on
next page).

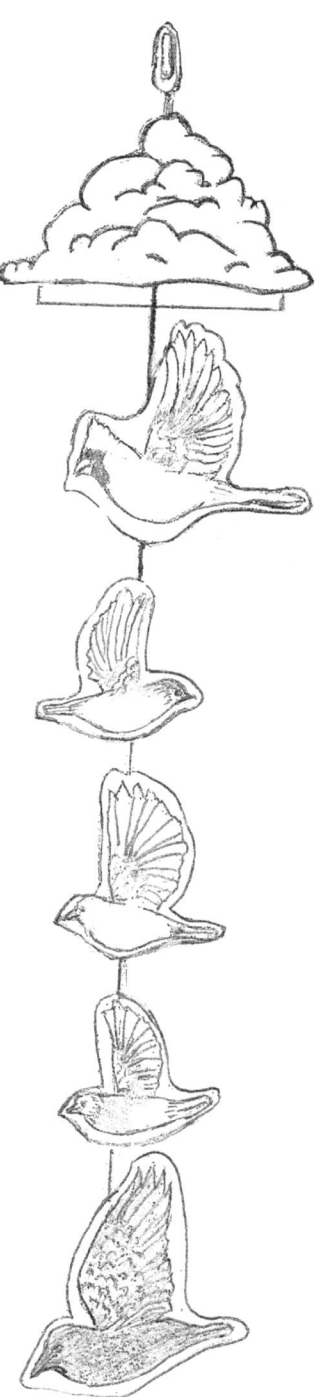

CARDINAL
WESTERN BLUE BIRD
WILSON'S WARBLER
EASTERN BLUEBIRD
BLACK BIRD

1ˢᵗ MOBILE HANGING GUIDELINES

Color, cut out birds (front and back ones), and cut out the clouds.

PLACE NEWSPAPER OR WAX PAPER UNDER WORK AREA!

1. Write artist name on the space below the clouds.
   Tie the top of the yarn to the paper clip!

2. Straighten out the long yarn (32 inches) where all the birds can dry over night.

3. Put weights on the yarn so it stays rather straight.

4. See next page of directions for the CLOUD - the Paper Clip is tied on first then the cloud glued on.

5. With the glue bottle point, carefully squirt glue onto yarn where the bird touches yarn. NOTICE WHERE THE YARN IS BEHIND THE BIRDS SO IT HANGS STRAIGHT!

6. Press Cardinal into place on the yarn.

7. Finish each of the birds that way.

   LET THE GLUE DRY OVER NIGHT!

8. NEXT DAY - Turn the mobile over, pull off from wax paper and glue back of birds & cloud in place.

   WHEN ALL GLUE IS DRY, HANG TO CELEBRATE ART WORK!

GLUE BOTH
SIDES TO
CARDBOARD

FRONT

GLUE
TO
YARN

Go over Cloud lines with Blue Pencil or Crayon.
Write Artist's Name in the box below the Cloud.

BACK

ADD CLOUD
BACK AND
BIRD BACKS
LAST

MOUNTAIN BLUEBIRD

COLOR BLUE

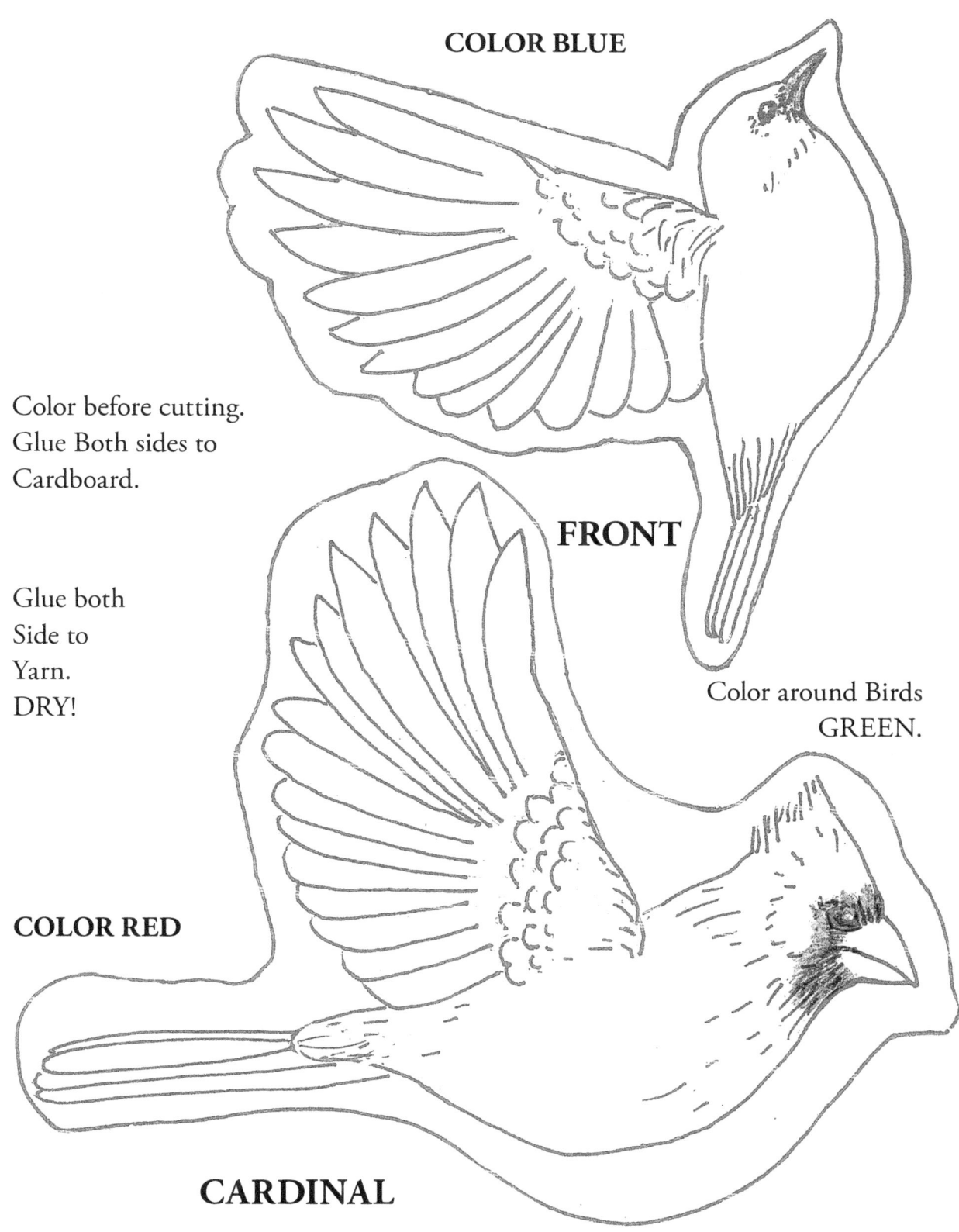

Color before cutting.
Glue Both sides to
Cardboard.

FRONT

Glue both
Side to
Yarn.
DRY!

Color around Birds
GREEN.

COLOR RED

CARDINAL

MOUNTAIN BLUEBIRD

COLOR BLUE

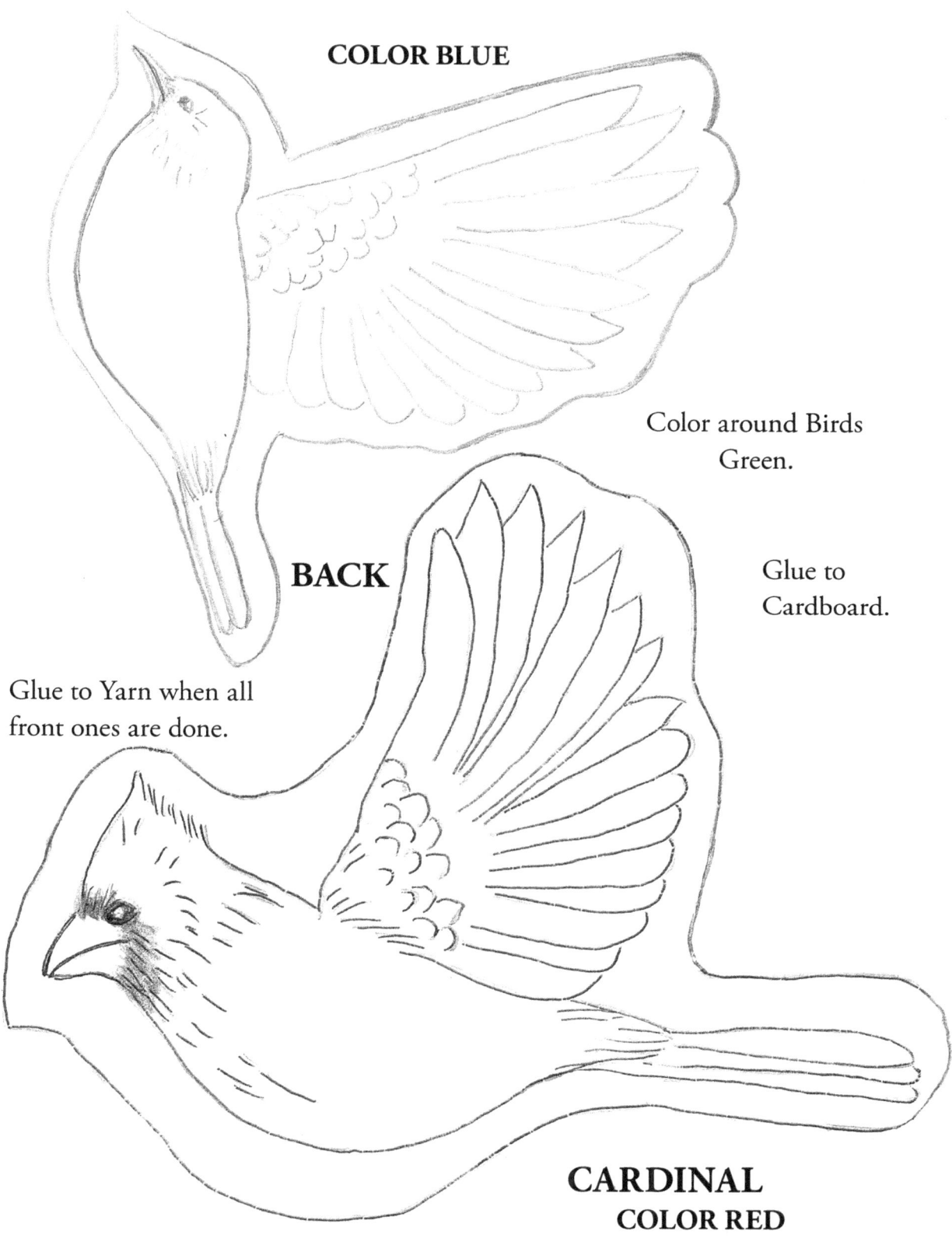

Color around Birds
Green.

BACK

Glue to
Cardboard.

Glue to Yarn when all
front ones are done.

CARDINAL
COLOR RED

AMERICAN CROW

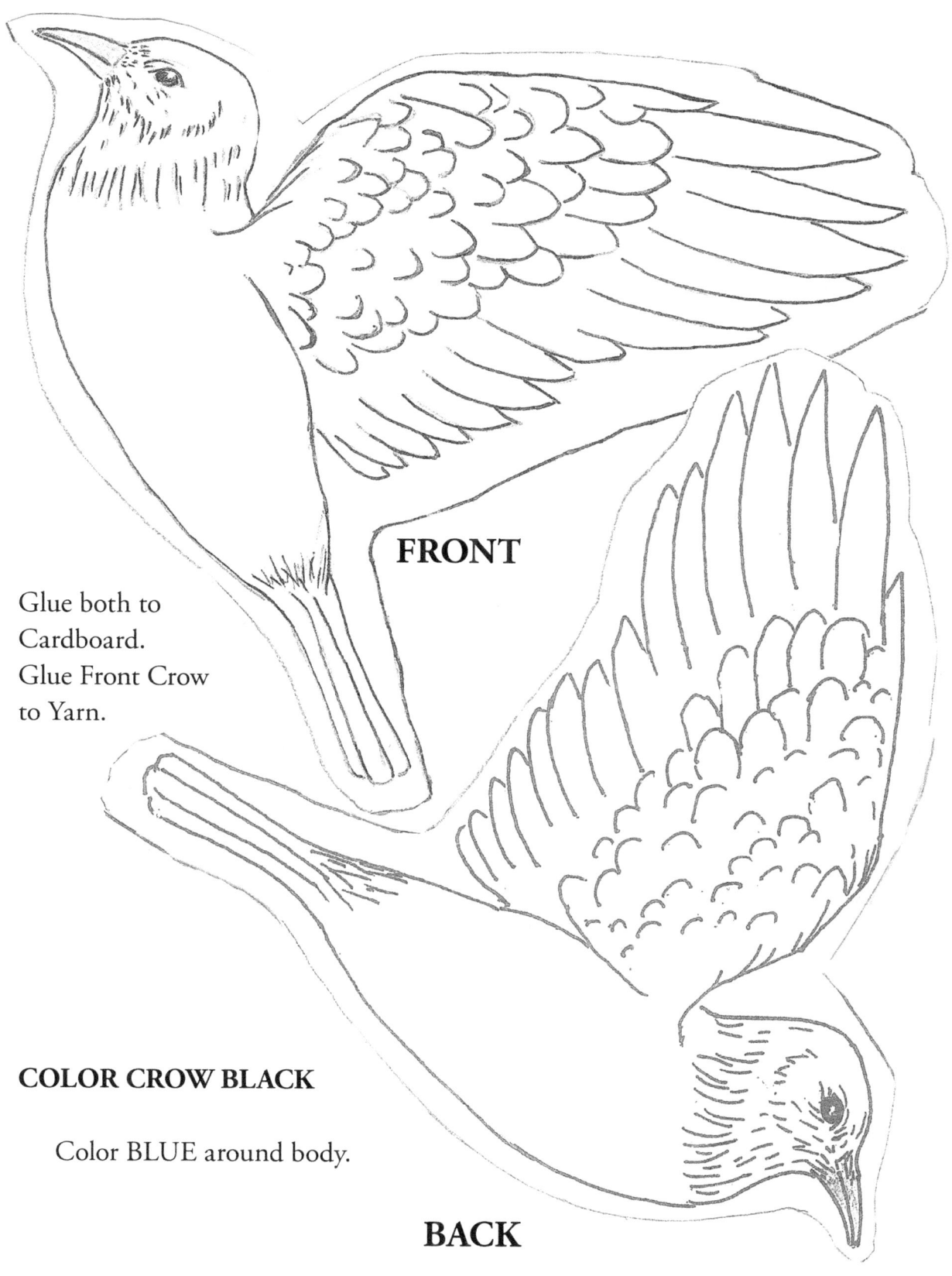

FRONT

Glue both to
Cardboard.
Glue Front Crow
to Yarn.

COLOR CROW BLACK

Color BLUE around body.

BACK

WILSON'S WARBLER

**COLOR WARBLER
YELLOW**

FRONT

Color around Warbler
Green.

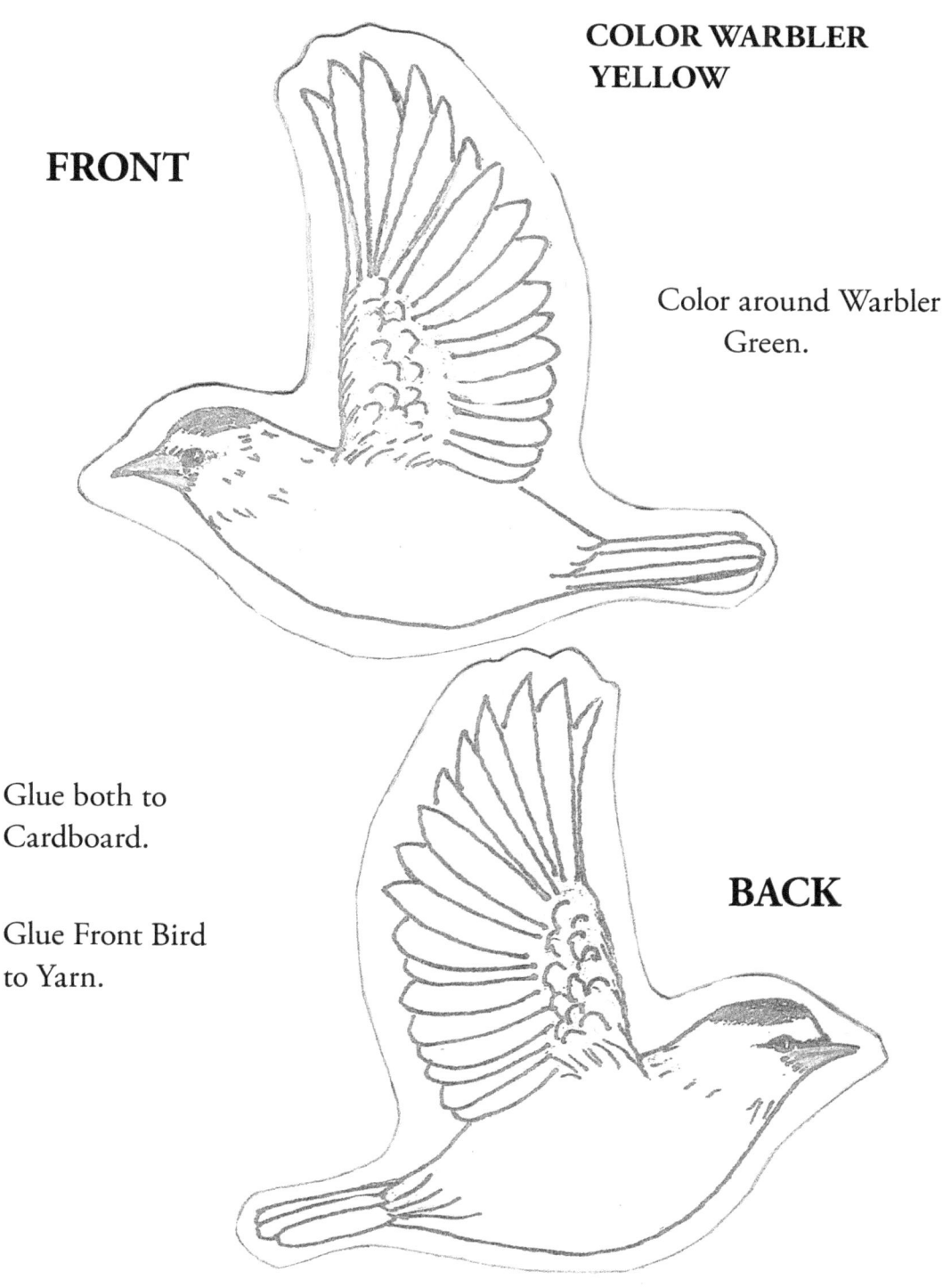

Glue both to
Cardboard.

Glue Front Bird
to Yarn.

BACK

EASTERN BLUEBIRD

Color before cutting.

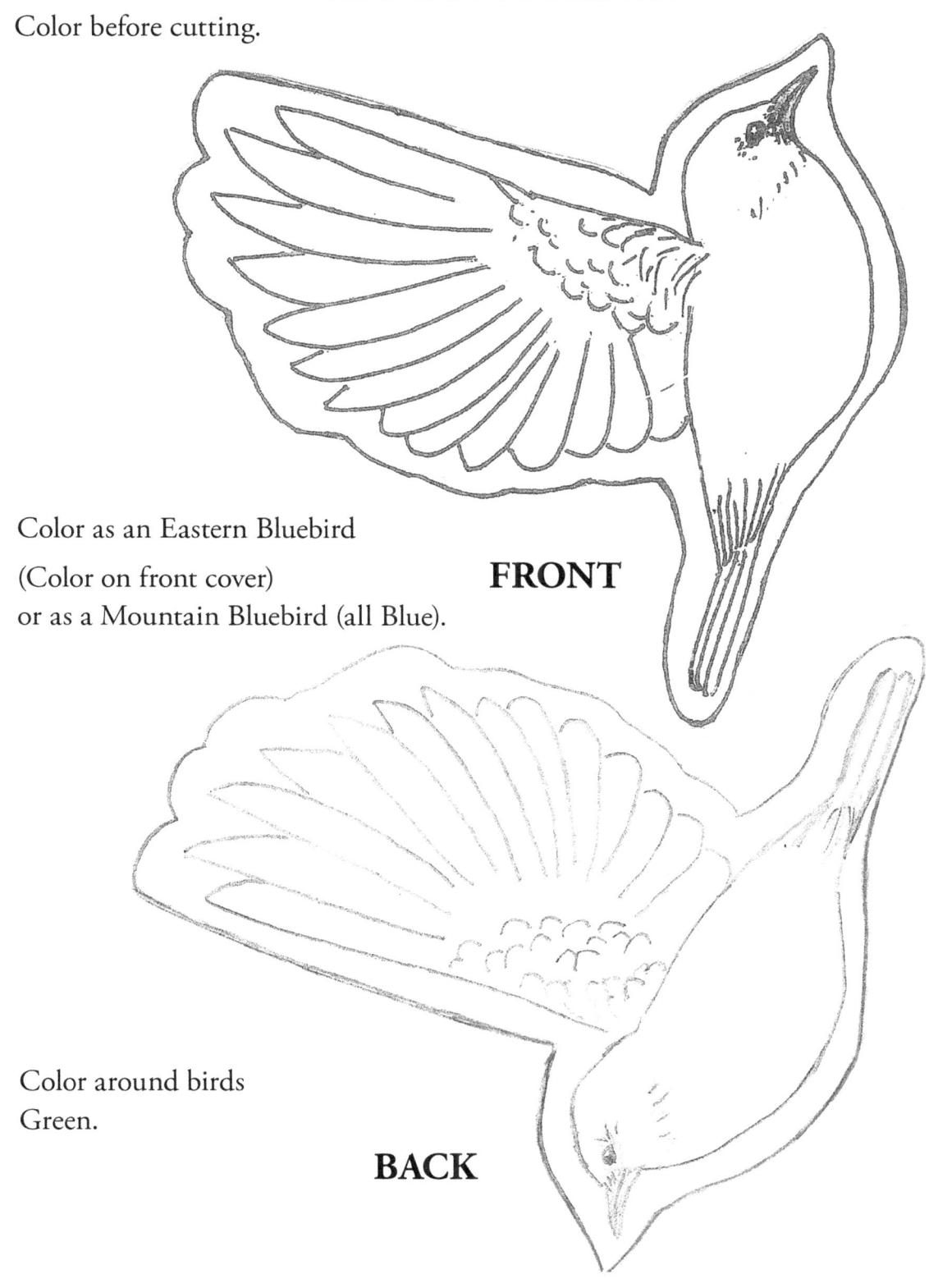

Color as an Eastern Bluebird

(Color on front cover)
or as a Mountain Bluebird (all Blue).

FRONT

Color around birds
Green.

BACK

CHAPTER 3

BUILD 1ST TOY BLUEBIRD HOUSE

To add Doorway to
Toy Bluebird House
cut out the circled
Doorway with Baby
Bluebirds on the
Back Cover.
Glue to the
House Front.

NEED: TISSUE BOX AND PIZZA BOX,
CRAYONS, SCISSORS,
TUBE AND LIQUID GLUE, TAPE

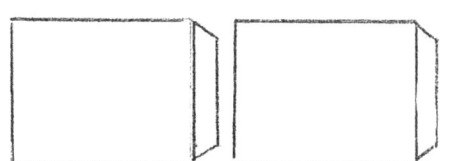

1. Cut tissue box in half
   (with opening at Top)

2. Push the boxes
   together,
   making one box.

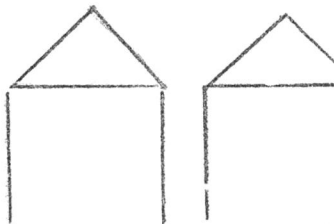
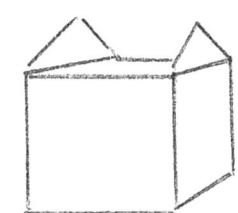

3. Copy Pattern (below) 2 times on
   cardboard. Cut out cardboard
   and glue to each end of the box.

4. Dry on each end, adding weight to
   be smooth. Cut edges to match box.

PATTERN GUIDE
CUT OUT

DRAW AROUND IT
2 TIMES ON
CARDBOARD.

CUT OUT BOTH.

USE LIQUID GLUE AROUND EDGES
AND DOWN THE CENTER.
TUBE GLUE ON THE REST.

Now that you have the Front and Back
pattern glued to the House, you are
ready to decorate your House.

Depending on the size
of your tissue box,
you may have longer decorative panels —
these are the outside walls with
windows and doors.
Tuck the longer bottom underneath
the box and glue and smooth.

The final corner strips
can be glued on to cover any
uneven house corners.

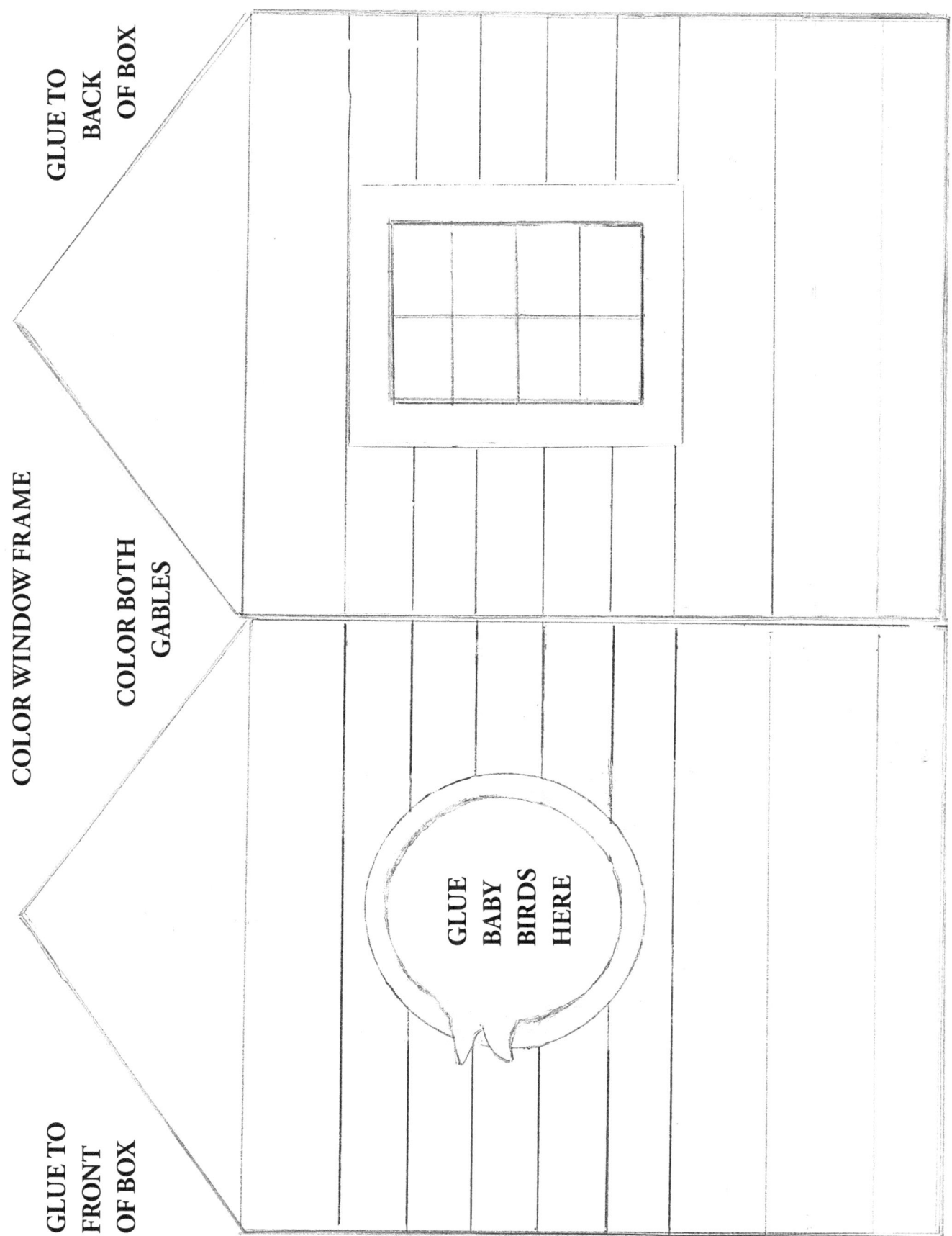

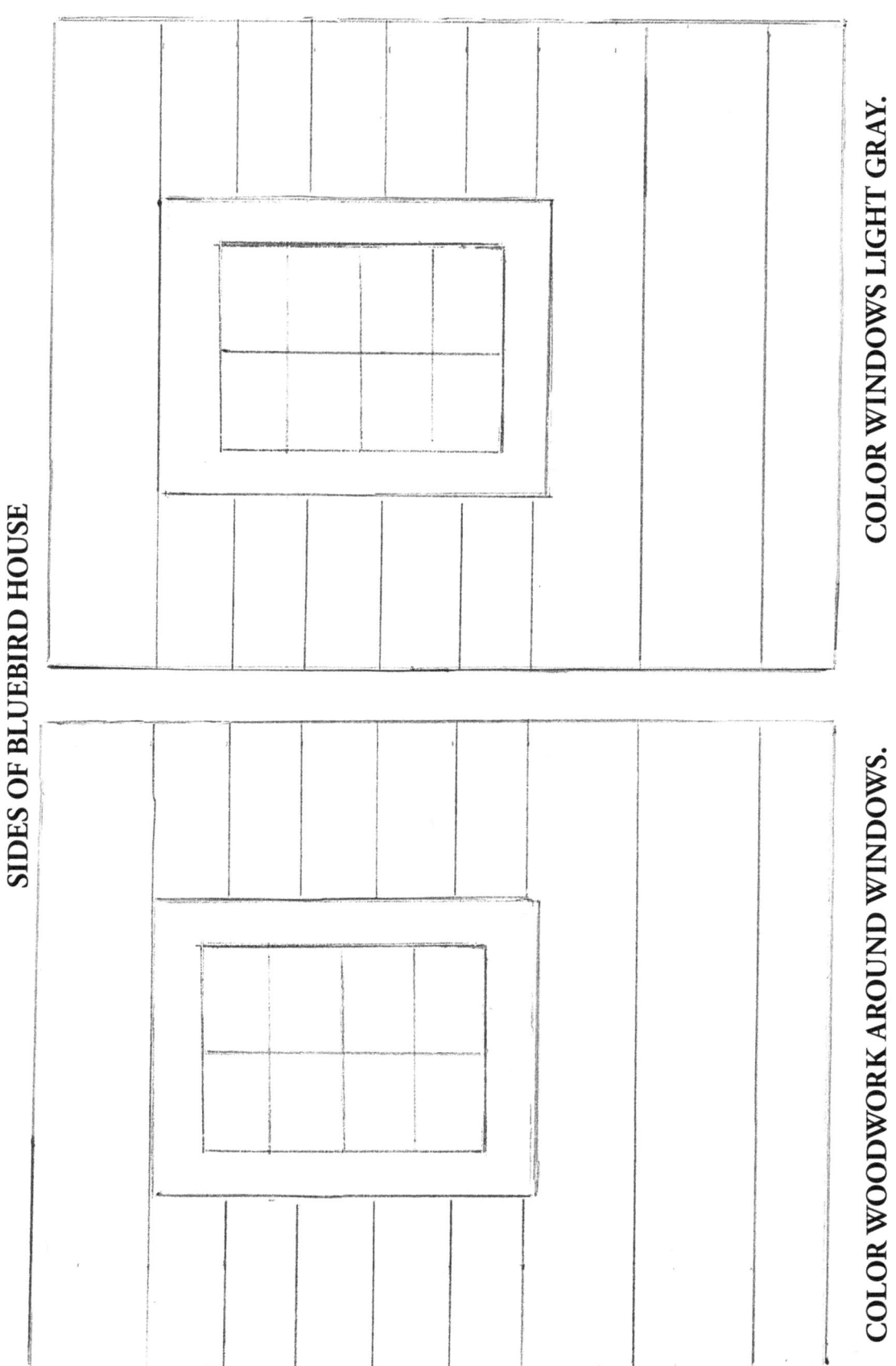

SIDES OF BLUEBIRD HOUSE

COLOR WINDOWS LIGHT GRAY.

FOLD AND GLUE EXTRA LENGTH TO BOTTOM

COLOR WOODWORK AROUND WINDOWS.

GLUE EACH SIDE ONTO HOUSE.

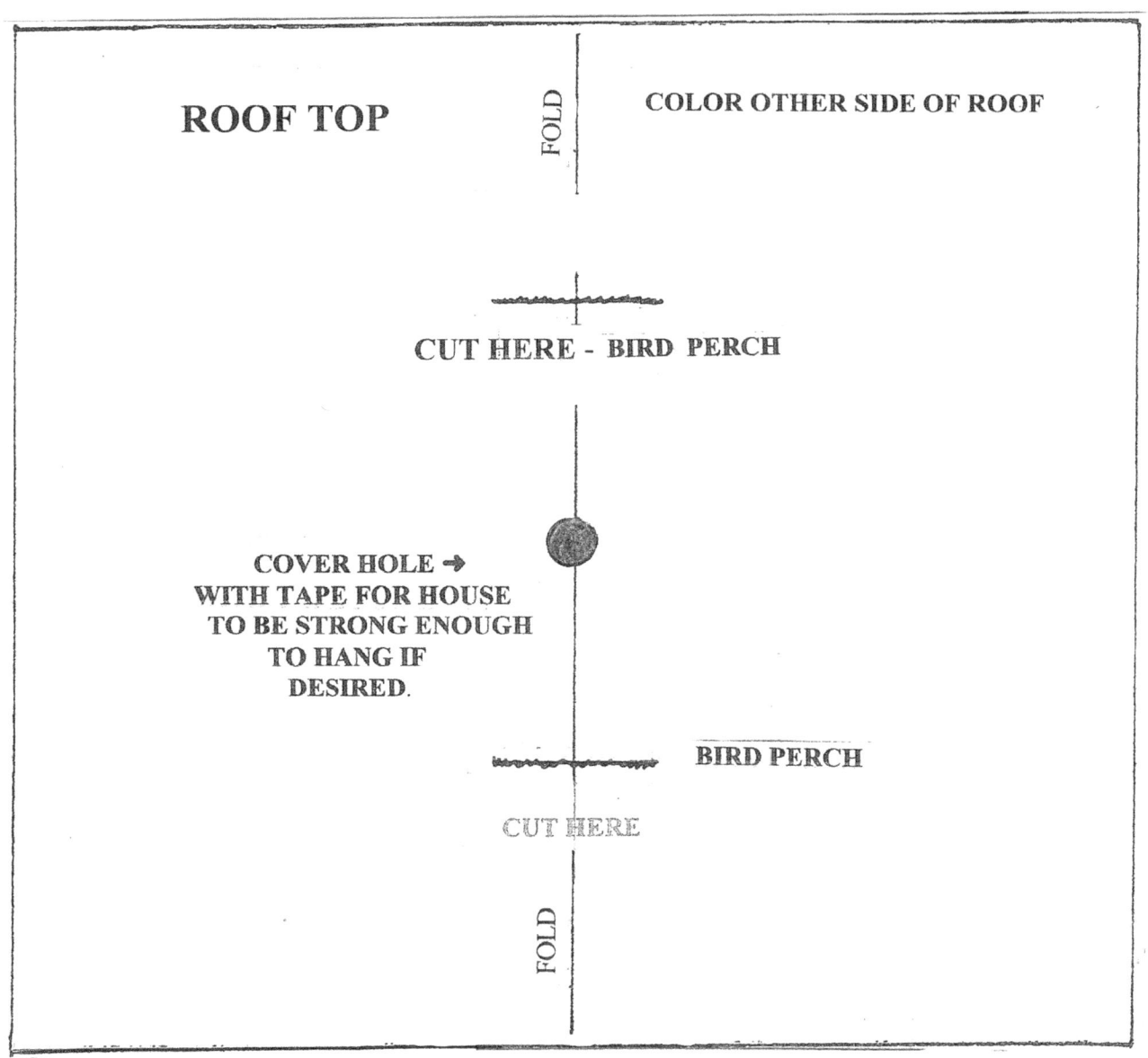

ROOF TOP

FOLD

COLOR OTHER SIDE OF ROOF

CUT HERE - BIRD PERCH

COVER HOLE →
WITH TAPE FOR HOUSE
TO BE STRONG ENOUGH
TO HANG IF
DESIRED.

BIRD PERCH

CUT HERE

FOLD

ROOF PATTERN

CUT OUT ROOF. TURN ROOF OVER AND COLOR.
GLUE ROOF TO CARDBOARD. DRY.
FOLD ON CENTER LINE.
CUT SMALL SLICES FOR BIRDS TO REST ON.
GLUE TO TOP OF TOY BLUEBIRD HOUSE.

BLUEBIRD HOUSE CORNER STRIPS COLOR ALL GREEN.

Color Bluebird House corner strips to match Gable color.
Cut out and fold on dotted line.
Glue onto corners of house.

BLUEBIRD HOUSE LABEL

TOY BLUEBIRD HOUSE

Made By: _____

Date: _____

Age: _____

Glue Label to House Bottom

CHAPTER 4

PARENT BLUEBIRDS

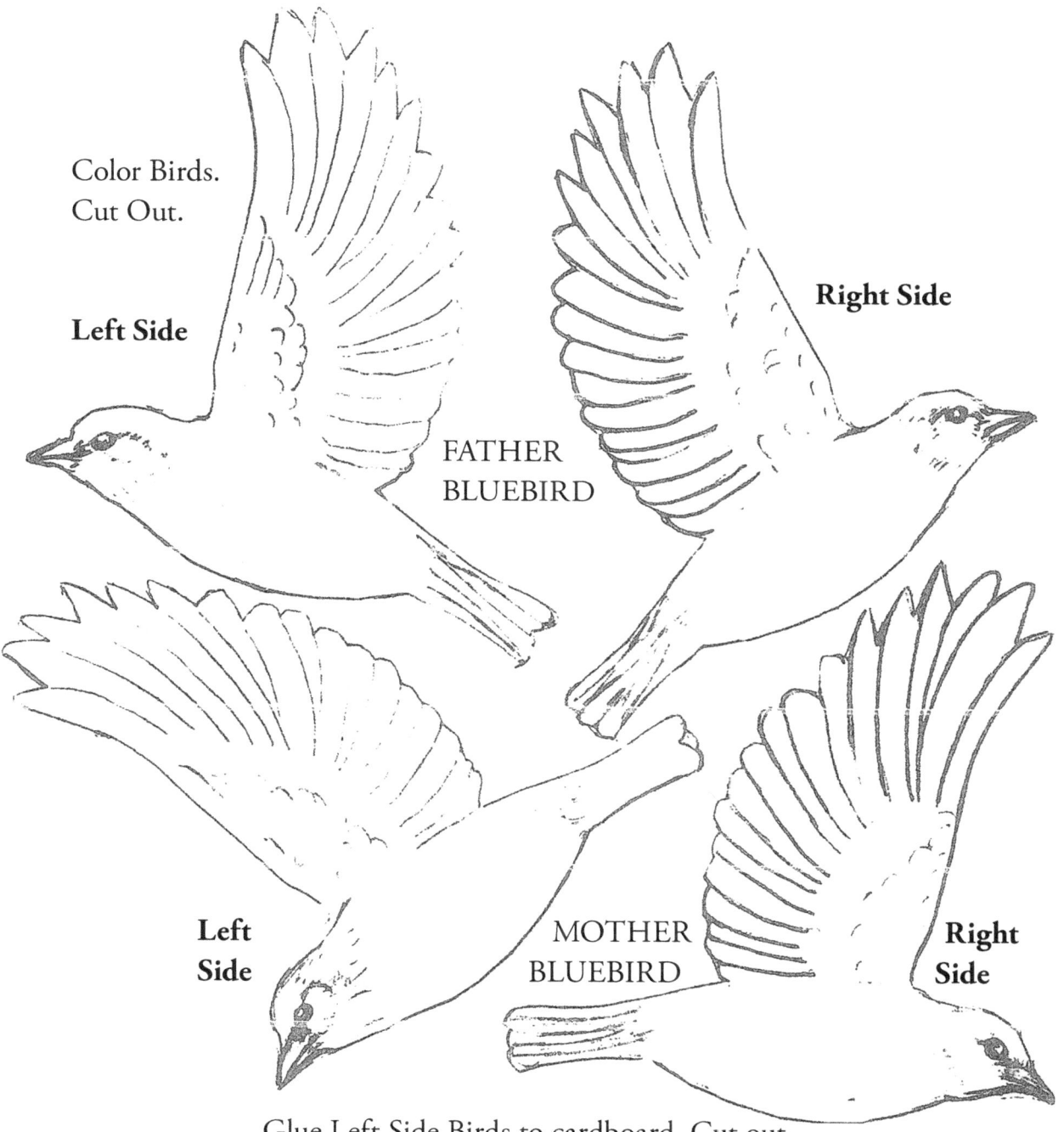

Color Birds.
Cut Out.

Left Side

Right Side

FATHER
BLUEBIRD

**Left
Side**

MOTHER
BLUEBIRD

**Right
Side**

Glue Left Side Birds to cardboard. Cut out.
Glue Right Side Birds to separate cardboard. Cut out.
Fold Wings outward from Body just a bit.

FATHER
BLUEBIRD

Color.
Cut out.
Glue.

TOP SIDE
OF
WINGS

MOTHER
BLUEBIRD

Color.
Cut out.
Glue.

Father Bluebird's two wings - color Blue.
Mother Bluebird's two wings - color Light Blue
Cut out. Test each wing to see how it fits, trim.
Glue Tops of wings in Place. Dry.
Glue Left and Right Bird Bodies together,
clamp with clothes pins until dry.

**Now the Bluebirds are ready for play action! When not playing, rest birds
on the roof of the Bluebird House in the two slots for them.**

RESOURCES

BIRDHOUSE FOR THE YARD
HOW TO BUILD A BLUEBIRD BOX
http://www.audubon.org/newa/diy-build-bluebird-box

BIRD WATCHING BOOK
https://www.audubon.org/birdguide
Great pictures of birds for children to see.

RIVER OF WORDS
YOUTH ART & POETRY CONTEST - AGES 5 TO 19.
www.stmarys-ca.edu/row
CHECK THE DATES FOR THE CONTEST!

THE AUTHOR/ARTIST

Devoted to creative work all her life: Patrice recalls making her own paper dolls; painting birds in the First Grade; creating posters for high school dances; sculpture skills developed along with print making and painting in college. Sculptures involved creating and casting abstract concrete, bronze and aluminum forms. Then on to high-fired porcelain abstracts and wildlife forms.

As a teacher, she encouraged students to enter the international River of Words art contest that involved the environment - with two winners! Another art student won First Place in the Arkansas River Art Contest. When serving as a Trustee on the Town Board, Patrice made the suggestion for the Town to become a Bird Sanctuary with local artists creating both summer and winter bird renditions for the Town sign.

For the Town Hall, her town teen students created three murals telling the history of the 1882 town. A gifted/talented students' project was a census mural of early state population. Another mural for a County welcome sign was for those who enjoyed boating, fishing, camping and enjoying the beach. Wonder what's next?

Now, art activity books and her own studio work is keeping her busy.